real love

can wait

[lessons for teen girls]

by Jaclynn Weber

© 2011
CHRISTIAN WOMANHOOD
A DIVISION OF PREPARE NOW RESOURCES
507 State Street
Hammond, Indiana 46320
www.christianwomanhood.org
(219) 932-0711

ISBN: 978-0-9845961-2-6

CREDITS:
Page Layout: Linda Stubblefield
Cover Design: Suzanna Cranston
Proofreaders: Rena Fish, Linda Flesher,
Jane Grafton, Cindy Schaap, Linda Stubblefield
Photography: Amy Luarca

Printed and Bound in the United States

real love can wait

{lessons for teen girls}

by Jaclynn Weber

Other Books
by Jaclynn Weber

Dedication

I would like to dedicate this book to my four sweet children whom I love with all my heart.

I am so thankful that God gave you to your father and I. We could not possibly be more happy to have you in our family.

- Lyndsay, I love your sweet spirit and your servant's heart.
- Raymond, you are so loving and very helpful to me.
- Alexys, you are a bundle of fun, and I love to hear you laugh.

- To our baby, I love you already, and I am thankful that God has given us another little boy.

Your dad and I pray daily that you will love the Lord with all of your hearts and that you will serve Him with all of your lives. I know God has a special plan for each of you. I am so excited to see what He will do through you.

I hope and pray that you will always stay close to Him. I love you, and I will always be proud to be called your mom.

– Jaclynn Weber

Acknowledgments

I WOULD LIKE TO thank Linda Stubblefield for her countless hours of hard work and her dedication to her job. She has been responsible for assembling each book I have written, not to mention the layout, several of the cover designs, and the editing and proofreading. She is definitely one of the hardest workers I know.

I would also like to thank Rena Fish, who has proofread each of my books, for her excellent work and attention to detail. Also, I would like to thank my mom, Cindy Schaap, Linda Flesher, and Jane Grafton for their help with the proofreading of this book.

Thank you to the media department of First Baptist Church for their work on the cover of this book. I appreciate their work and dedication.

I would like to thank Amy Luarca for allowing me to use her photographs in this book.

"Sow a thought,
reap an action;

Sow an action,
reap a habit;

Sow a habit,
reap a character;

Sow a character;
reap a destiny."

–*C. Reade*

About the Author

JACLYNN WEBER IS the wife of Brother Todd Weber, the junior high youth pastor at First Baptist Church of Hammond, Indiana. She is the only daughter of Pastor and Mrs. Jack Schaap.

Mrs. Weber is a 2002 graduate of Hyles-Anderson College. At graduation she received the coveted "Miss Hylander" award.

Jaclynn is the author of six additional books which have been written specifically to teenage young ladies. Mrs. Weber is an often-requested conference speaker. At First Baptist Church where she is very involved in the music program, Jaclynn serves as one of three pianists. Jaclynn also assists her husband with the eighth grade Sunday school department and the junior high teen church on Sunday mornings.

10 | Real Love Can Wait

Married on June 1, 2002, the Webers are the parents of Lyndsay, Raymond, Alexys, and one on the way.

Table of Contents

Introduction

FALLING IN LOVE WITH JESUS
"I am my beloved's, and my beloved is mine...."
(Song of Solomon 6:3)

A radiant bride greeted her guests with a brilliant smile as she entered the reception hall after the wedding ceremony. She gracefully moved about the room, the train of her white gown flowing along the floor behind her, her veil cascading down her button-adorned back.

She conversed with each guest one by one, taking the time to mingle and soak up the compliments. "You look absolutely lovely." "Your dress is divine." "I've never seen a more beautiful bride." "What a stunning ceremony." The lavish praises rang on and on. The bride couldn't have been more proud or more appreciative of the crowd's adoration. She could have listened to them swoon over her all evening. As a matter of fact, she did.

But where was the groom? All the attention focused on the bride, and never once did she call anyone's attention to her husband. She didn't even notice his absence at her side. Scanning the room, I searched for him, wondering, "Where could he be?"

I finally found him, but not where I expected him to be. The groom stood alone in the corner of the room with his head down. As he stared at his ring, twisting the gold band that his bride had just placed on his finger, tears trickled down his cheeks and onto his hands. That is when I noticed the nail scars. The groom was Jesus.

He waited, but the bride never once turned her face toward her groom. She never held His hand. She never introduced the guests to Him. She operated independently of Him.

I awoke with a sick feeling in my stomach, realizing

that I'd been dreaming. "Lord, is this how I made You feel when I was looking for love in all the wrong places?" I wept at the thought of hurting Him so deeply.

Unfortunately, this dream illustrates exactly what is happening between God and millions of His people. He betroths Himself to us; we take His name, and then we go about our lives looking for love, attention, and affection from every source under the sun except from the Son of God, the Lover of our souls.

Oh, how Jesus longs for us to acknowledge Him, to introduce Him to our friends, to withdraw to be alone with Him, to cling to Him for our identity, to gaze longingly into His eyes, and to love Him with all our heart and soul.

What about you? Do you have this kind of love relationship with Christ? Do you experience the incredible joy of intimacy with the One Who loves you with a passion that is far deeper, far greater than anything you could find here on earth? We know from experience that you can.

by Shannon Ethridge & Stephen Arterburn

"THE ANCESTOR OF EVERY ACTION
IS A THOUGHT."

–*R. W. Emerson*

"THOUGHT IS THE SCULPTOR
WHO CAN CREATE
THE PERSON YOU WANT TO BE."

–*H. D. Thoreau*

CHAPTER ONE

Real Love Can Wait

When I was in grade school, there was a little chant that we girls would say when a boy liked a girl. (I'll just use some pretend names for this chapter!) We would chant the following rhyme,

> Billy and Sarah sittin' in a tree—
> K-i-s-s-i-n-g.
> First comes love, then comes marriage,
> Then comes Sarah with a baby carriage!

My friends and I would chant that rhyme to each other and laugh and laugh. However, if the person being chanted about was listening, he or she would probably deny the "accusation" and run off with a bright red face from embarrassment—but knowing inside that the person really did like whom we were chanting about! It was just a silly little poem, but there was actually some truth to it. God does want a couple to love first, then marry, and then have children. God's plan is so simple that even a child can understand this concept. The world has a very different view of love though. Through television and Hollywood, children and teens and, yes, even adults are being taught that first comes a physical relationship, then maybe living together for a while to see if they are compatible enough for each other. They may even have a few children if the children do not interfere with a career. Perhaps someday they will eventually settle down and finally marry each other. The world's philosophy does not fit very well in that little chant, nor does it fit the plan that God intended when He created man.

The problem with this worldly philosophy is that everything is based on selfishness. I have read some quotes written by young men and published in a teen magazine. These young men were sharing what they wanted in a girlfriend. Most of the items on the list addressed how the girls made them feel, how they fit into their schedules, and how they met their needs. Everything these young men wanted in a girlfriend centered on them, with no thought about what the girls needed or wanted.

In I John 2:16, the Bible describes very well what the world's view of love is: *"...the lust of the flesh, and the lust of the eyes, and the pride of life...."* Without God, there can be no love for God is the source of love. If Christians are going to learn how to love, they must first get their love from God.

While I was in college, I remember my Grandpa Hyles preaching a sermon about two types of love:

Phileo Love

Phileo love is a fondness or an attraction for something. If I say, "I love ice cream!" I mean that I like ice cream a lot. It does not mean I have a deep relationship and an abiding love for my ice cream. Ice cream is simply something I enjoy.

Agape Love

Agape love is a deep, abiding love that is unconditional and never changes, regardless of the circumstances. This love is the love most parents have for a child, the love a soldier has for his country, and the love that Jesus has for us. This love never goes away because it comes from an eternal and unending source. John 15:13, *"Greater love hath no man than this, that a man lay down his life for his friends."*

We now know that true love, agape love, comes only from God, but there are also different levels of love. Let me explain. When I was in kindergarten, I liked a boy (whom I will call John). (I probably had a boyfriend in the nursery, but kindergarten is the first one I can remember! I always liked a boy or had a crush on someone!) I fell down at the playground one day, and John helped me up, so for a while, he was the love of my life! Now as a five-year-old, I did not have very much love to give to John, so our relationship did not last very long—probably less than a day! If I had given John all of the love my little heart could have held, it would probably have equaled about a drop of water in a bucket! This is an example of phileo love, which does not go very deep. I think John and I liked each other for maybe a whole day.

When I was in the sixth grade, I liked another boy whom I will call Bill (and there were quite a few in between). Bill and I were serious! I mean, every day we would walk down the hallway to the lunch counter together and help sell sandwiches—that's practically going steady! Bill was a very nice boy, and I liked him for a while. I did have a little more love to give him than I had to give to John as a kindergartner, but if my love were water, it was probably not enough to fill even a measuring cup! We definitely did not have enough love to keep us together or to make it through a lifetime of love and commitment to each other.

In eighth grade I liked another boy, and we went to the Valentine banquet together. He was in high school, and his taking me to the banquet was a big deal for me as a junior higher. I thought this high schooler was really neat. Again, we liked each other for a while. I was a Christian, so my love was growing and becoming deeper. Still, I did not have enough love to withstand the tests and trials of life. Both of us eventually moved on to liking other people. Each time I liked a boy, the love

I had for him was real and came from God, but my love was not mature enough to even think of getting serious or marrying someone yet. It still had a long way to go to become the deep, abiding love that I would one day give to my husband.

I dated some in high school, and I even became quite serious with one particular guy whom I liked very much and with whom I felt I was in love. He and I dated for quite a while until we realized that God had a different plan for our lives. Though I felt like I was in love, I was not yet ready to settle down and give all of my love to just one person. My love was still not mature. God had some more work to do in teaching me how to love someone with all of my heart.

Yes, the love I had was real, but to give the love I had to one person at that point in my life would not have been fair to anyone. I was not yet ready to love someone unconditionally; I was not yet ready to make sacrifices and love someone completely. Now if the love I had then was water, it would probably have quenched someone's thirst for a little while, but it would eventually have run out because I did not have enough love to last a lifetime.

During the time between high school and college, I began to really pray and even fast for the person God had for me. God began working in my heart. I believe it was during this time that God wanted me to mature and grow in His love so that I would be able to love someone completely and unconditionally…and forever. It was during my freshman year of college when I would finally meet HIM, the man of my dreams. This man would be the one I would marry and with whom I would spend the rest of my life. My love was finally ready, finally mature enough to give away completely, and this time it was different.

The love I had for Todd Weber never ran out; it kept on coming and coming. It was as if I were underneath a waterfall of love that never ran dry but kept giving and giving. The more love I gave, the more I had to give. Where did all of that love come from? Of course, it was God's love pouring out through me to the man I would one day call my husband, my lover, and my best friend.

God had prepared us for each other, and when the time was right, He gave us all the love our hearts could desire and the deep, abiding love that would last forever. He filled us with His love, and His well of love never runs dry. It lasts through trials, through testing, and through loss and heartache. God's love grows stronger and stronger all the time. God's love never ends.

You, too, have a measure of love that God has given to you which you will one day give to that special person whom God has chosen for you. The problem comes when we get too anxious and give our love away before it has had a chance to mature and grow. We soon find out that it was not enough to sustain us. This lack causes intense pain and heartbreak and often the loss of a relationship. A girl who decides to give her heart away as a teenager will often do anything for a guy, but she usually ends up with an overwhelming feeling of loss and loneliness when she realizes that the guy she thought she loved did not love her or when she realizes that her love was not strong enough to last. Often though, this realization is not thought of until a girl's purity is taken away or a child is conceived. At that point comes an intense amount of guilt and remorse.

It takes a tree many, many years to grow from the time it starts as a seed, and so it takes time for your love to mature. When love is ready, there will be an unending supply, and you will feel happier than you have ever felt in your life. True love is more wonderful than any other feeling in the world, and you can have it if you will just be patient—real love can wait!

Song of Solomon 8:6, 7, *"Set me as a seal upon thine heart, as a seal upon thine arm: for love is strong as death; jealousy is cruel as the grave: the coals thereof are coals of fire, which hath a most vehement flame. Many waters cannot quench love, neither can the floods drown it: if a man would give all the substance of his house for love, it would utterly be contemned."*

"A SINGLE BAD HABIT WILL MAR
AN OTHERWISE FAULTLESS CHARACTER,
AS AN INK-DROP SOILETH
THE PURE WHITE PAGE."

–H. Ballou

"EVERY TIME THE CHRISTIAN SUCCUMBS
TO THE SINFUL OPTION OF TEMPTATION,
HE FIGURATIVELY POINTS HIS FINGER AT GOD
AND SAYS, 'YOU ARE NOT ENOUGH FOR ME!' "

–J. Schaap

CHAPTER TWO

Purity Is an Issue of the Heart

"He that loveth pureness of heart, for the grace of his lips the king shall be his friend."
(Proverbs 22:11)

Being pure and staying pure is not a matter of just saving your body for your wedding night, although that is extremely important. Purity covers a whole variety of areas: it is a mentality, an action, an attitude, an act of self-control, and a decision of the heart. There are many girls who may have "saved themselves" for their wedding night, but their hearts and minds are far from pure. Many girls are still moral simply because they have not had the opportunity to do wrong, because they are too scared of what might happen to them, or because they don't want to risk becoming pregnant. However, what these girls think about and how they act are not at all what God intended when He created them in His image.

Have you ever baked cookies without the eggs? I have, and they did not turn out very well! Have you ever tried to sew something without using a pattern? Well, if you did, I doubt if it turned out very well (unless you are an amazing seamstress, unlike myself!). Have you ever tried to drive somewhere you have never been without using a GPS or getting directions? Well, if you did, then you probably got lost! I've done that more times than I can count! What about shopping without taking money or a credit card? I doubt that the sales clerk at the counter let you buy anything for "free." I don't think that stores sell clothes for charity, at least not the last time I checked!

May I share a story about a beautiful young girl who had big dreams for herself and for her life. She grew up in church, and she loved God and the Bible. She had many Christian friends who loved the Lord like she did.

She was reared in a good family and was surrounded by all of the "right things." There were no televisions to corrupt her mind, no cell phones to send filthy pictures, no Internet to set up a "myspace.com" type of Web site, and no perverted movies or DVDs to rent from RedBox or to download; yet, she still managed to corrupt her life and the lives of her family members.

She grew up loving God, and she even married a Godly Christian man who was devoted to God as well as to his wife. They were madly in love and enjoyed several wonderful years together serving God. Then one day, they decided that God's will wasn't as great as they had once thought. Times were tough, and money was scarce, so they decided to do their own thing and move away from God's will. They soon discovered how difficult it was to love God while living in the world. Before they knew it, they were living a worldly, godless life of self. They lived for the now and wanted bigger and better, but it never brought the happiness they once had. They were confused. Their confusion only pulled them further from the God they once knew. They did everything they could to be happy, yet the parties and friends never filled the void that was always gnawing at their hearts.

Then one day, the worst happened. The wife came home from work to find her husband dead. She was in shock! He had become a pretty rough guy, but she never thought she would come home to find him dead. Had he turned his back on someone and that person had killed him? Had he become so miserable in sin that he took his own life? She did not know how he died, but she did understand that she had just lost the only man she had ever loved more than life itself.

To make matters even worse, shortly after the death of her husband, her two sons were also killed while out "living it up." She was beside herself with grief. God had seemingly taken away the people who were dearest to her, and now she had no idea what she was going to do. This distraught lady became angry and bitter at God, blaming Him for every problem she had ever had. "Why would a so-called loving God do such cruel things to me?" she wondered. "If He is so good, then why do such horrible things happen?" She just could not understand.

After many months of intense pain and bitterness in her heart, she finally realized that she needed God. She acknowledged that it was through her foolishness and her family's sin that the ones she loved were taken. She realized that God still and always would love her unconditionally. So, she decided to pack her bags and move back home where God was first place in her life and where she knew she would find true happiness. So she came back to God, to her home, to her family, and to everything she once knew. For the first time in many years, she felt truly happy.

This story is in the Bible (I may have "changed" it a little!), but it is the story of a woman named Naomi and her journey back to God. Just as it is impossible to bake something without all the right ingredients, and just as a person will get lost without the right directions, and just as Naomi learned that without God one cannot have true happiness, one cannot be pure if he has an immoral heart.

A pure heart is one of the necessary ingredients to having a pure life. If your heart is not *"...washed from filthiness"* as the Bible instructs, then you are not a pure teenager. You may not have been immoral with a guy yet, but you are not pure in God's eyes. Being pure in God's eyes is just as important as saving your body for your husband.

Ask God daily to give you a pure heart. Every day you need to confess your sins and ask Him to help you to stay pure. Having a pure heart is really quite simple. Ask God to give you one and to keep you from doing things that would defile it! Having a pure heart is the first step in staying pure until your wedding day.

CHAPTER THREE

Stay in the Castle

I once read a story written by Pastor Jerry Ross, entitled *Stay in the Castle*. He wrote this story for a teenage girl who was on his bus route when he was a bus captain. This girl had met a boy at work and wanted to date him. However, the young man was neither a Christian nor a church goer. She had always wanted to be a missionary's wife and someday return to Mexico, her home country. This bus captain, in an attempt to keep her from ruining her life and destroying her dreams, wrote a story about a princess who lived with her father the king.

The king and his daughter lived in a beautiful castle, and the princess had everything she could ever wish for, yet what she really wanted was to go to the village and see how the "common people" lived. After meeting the delivery boy who brought parcels to the castle, she decided to sneak out one night, go to the village, and see life in the village for herself.

There she met the boy at a village event, walked with this boy, and eventually fell in love with him. After several months, she finally told her father she was leaving the castle for good. Her father, with tears in his eyes, watched her leave, knowing that she was making the worst decision of her life.

She later learned that the man she married was not everything he had promised to be. One day as she swept the dirt floor of their tiny hut, she looked toward the castle and saw a prince on a white horse riding to the castle entrance. She saw him knock on the door, talk to the king, sadly turn away, and then ride off into the distance. She brushed at her tear-filled eyes as she realized that the prince she saw was the man her father had told her would one day come. He had come for her, and she had missed him. At that moment, she realized her life would never be "happily ever after" again.

Stay in the Castle is an excellent story which is available to order. I would strongly recommend purchasing a copy of this wonderful booklet for your daughter. This story, though, is simply another attempt to help teenagers choose the right path and to help each of you realize how important those seemingly harmless choices can be.

In working with young people, I have told the story of *The Mysterious Alabaster Bottle** written by Elizabeth Rice Handford. This story is about a girl who nearly lost her purity but who, at the last moment, decided to wait and save herself for her husband. I have also told about the girl at school who was ridiculed for taking a stand because the girls who were immoral knew they had lost the valued and priceless possession of purity this girl had.

Satan is an expert at making the "village" life look so good. He knows exactly how to entice us at our weakest point until we surrender to his will. Then, like a vicious tiger or lion, he pounces on us and tells us how horrible and wretched we are. These kinds of stories are also seen over and over throughout the Bible. Some examples are as follows:

◆ The prodigal who left home for a better life returned a miserable man.

◆ Samson, who had everything, wanted Delilah, but she turned on him and caused his eventual destruction.

◆ David, who was in charge of the whole kingdom of Israel and who could have had any woman he wanted for his wife, wanted Bath-sheba because he was not content to "stay in the castle." He had to have her, and his life was forever changed.

Over and over in the Bible, as well as throughout history, we see those who were not content with what God gave them and those who had to experience the "village" life for themselves. Did you know that every time the results were the same? Life is not like the Hollywood movies where a girl who was destined for someone else falls in love with a so-called outcast where the couple lives happily ever after. That scenario may look appealing, but it does not work in reality.

If you are a Christian, then you had better date a Christian. If you have surrendered to full-time

Christian service, then you need to date someone who is surrendered as well. I beg those of you who seem to have it altogether but who, inside, are not content and are considering running away from the life you have been given, please, please don't leave God's will. Today, once again, I beg you to "stay in the castle." By the way, the girl to whom this story was written is now a missionary's wife in Mexico!

The booklet *Stay in the Castle* may be obtained by contacting Jerry and Sheryl Ross.

- Web site: www.stayinthecastle.com
- Email: ultimategoal@stayinthecastle.com
- Ultimate Goal Publications, 4969 W. CR 1200 S., Jasonville, Indiana 47438

*The Mysterious Alabaster Bottle may be obtained by visiting www.JoyfulChristianMinistries.com online.

"CHILDHOOD IS A TIME
OF CHARACTER BUILDING.
TEENAGE YEARS ARE A TIME
OF CHARACTER TESTING.
ADULTHOOD IS A TIME
OF CHARACTER REAPING."

–J. Hyles

CHAPTER FOUR

Is Your Texting Pure?

My family and I were sitting around the porch at my parents' house on Father's Day when I noticed my son Ray doing something that looked like typing or writing on a little board. I saw him look at his sister and say, "I'm busy texting!" When I asked him what he was doing, he said they were playing "Mommy and Daddy"! From that answer, I can only guess that he sees me texting a lot!

I do love texting! It is so easy and fast, and often you can accomplish more when you text than when you talk on the phone, especially when you are in a hurry. I have never been a big phone talker, so that is another reason for me to love texting.

The Bible says in Psalm 19:14, *"Let the words of my mouth, and the meditation of my heart, be acceptable in thy sight, O LORD, my strength, and my redeemer."* The Bible also says in I Corinthians 14:40, *"Let all things be done decently and in order."*

I know of a student who was expelled from school for some indecent behavior with the opposite gender. They were sending pictures of themselves to each other on their phones and texting wrong things back and forth. The "meditation of their hearts" was definitely not in the right place, and their pictures were definitely not taken "decently and in order."

Satan loves to take something that is totally harmless in itself and pervert it into something sinful. The Internet, for instance, is a very helpful research tool for those who are in school as well as a helpful shopping outlet. Yet Satan has used it to cause one of the biggest problems in our society today—the addiction to pornography. He has taken something very valuable and turned it into something very harmful. The same is true with texting and sending pictures on phones. There is nothing wrong with texting a friend or taking a photo to put on your wallpaper, but to take and send indecent photos of yourself to others is not only sinful, but it is very dangerous.

Please understand, girls, that when you stoop to a low level of sending indecent photos, you are proving how little you value yourself and your life. There are obviously more problems hidden underneath the surface because you need some help with feeling secure and confident in who you are as a Christian girl. You can and should get some Godly advice and some help to take you in the proper direction.

In Judges 19 an account is given of a Levite sojourner and his concubine journeying from Bethlehem-judah to the house of God where they were given a place to stay in Gibeah for a night. The Bible says that sons of Belial surrounded their host's house, beat at the door, and asked the host to send out the man for their pleasure. The host offered his daughter to the wicked men, and finally the Levite gave them his concubine. The wicked men abused her all night long, and when morning came, the Levite found her lying dead on the threshold of the house where he had spent the night. The

Levite then did a very strange thing. He cut her body into 12 pieces and sent the pieces to each of the 12 tribes of Israel as a warning that God would punish their nation if they did not obey God and live a pure and holy life. Judges 19:30 says, *"...consider of it, take advice...."*

Judges 19 is really a disgusting story and one that makes me cringe when I read it. Yet it is not so different from those who "sell" their bodies on the Internet and exchange ungodly and unholy pictures with others. When you do that, you are pretty much saying, "I am not worth as much as the Godly girls, so just do whatever you want with me." That thinking is very sad because your life and your body are sacred and precious to God. The Bible says to be holy. Being holy includes your texting as well as your physical purity. We are to keep our minds pure, not thinking about others in an inappropriate way. We are to keep our hearts pure, meditating and spending holy time with a holy God. We are to keep our bodies pure, staying as far away from immorality and the appearance of immorality as possible.

If God were on Facebook, would He be your

"friend"? Would you be totally comfortable with His reading and looking at everything on your page, OR would you be completely embarrassed and ashamed at the things He would see. Do you care what He thinks? You should because He has the power to give life and the power to take it and because He only puts up with sin for so long.

I know one thing: I am going to be very careful what I text and what I look at because as Hebrews 10:31 says, *"It is a fearful thing to fall into the hands of the living God."*

Let's make sure we honor God with everything we do, say, and think. I want Him to see my life and be glad He created me.

"DESTINY IS NO MATTER OF CHANCE.
IT IS A MATTER OF CHOICE:
IT IS NOT A THING TO BE WAITED FOR,
IT IS A THING TO BE ACHIEVED."

–W. J. Bryan

"CHARACTER IS NOT MADE IN A CRISIS—
IT IS ONLY EXHIBITED."

–R. Freeman

CHAPTER FIVE

Too Weak to Stand

At the time of this writing, my church has just finished one of the greatest Youth Conferences I think we've ever had! Funny skits, great preaching, beautiful fireworks, and an exciting bus demolition all helped to make it an incredible week. My favorite part, though, was the invitation after my dad's sermon, "America, America," on Friday afternoon. Nothing gives me more hope for our country than seeing young men and teenage guys surrendering to preach, to pray for our country, and to serve God with their lives. It is so encouraging to see men who want to serve God and do what is right and to see guys who have the courage and boldness to stand up for what they believe.

I also believe that girls, as well as guys, need to have boldness, courage, and confidence toward doing right and serving God. I was in a counseling session with a counselor who was talking to a single girl, and he talked about her having the courage to do the hard thing or the thing she knew was right but did not want to do. He said, "Girls are supposed to have guts, right?" The answer is YES! Girls are supposed to have the courage to do what is right just like guys are. I am not talking about boldness to make a mockery of God or what He stands for either. I'm talking about a resolve and a devotion to the Lord to do what is right—no matter what the cost.

When my daughter Alexys was two, she was the chubbiest of any of my kids! Her roly-poly legs and knees took a while to be able to hold up her body! She crawled pretty early, and sometimes she would try to pull herself up, but she would just plop right back down because her legs and tiny, fat feet were too weak to hold her up. She simply could not stand because her legs were not strong enough to hold her!

I think she illustrates a lot of teenage girls in fundamentalism today. These girls are beautiful and sweet on the outside, but when it comes to doing right, they are just too weak to stand. They cannot stand for right because their faith is not strong enough to sustain them. They believe in God, yet they have never completely attached themselves to Him; they want to stay pure and clean, but they have never practiced saying "no" to a guy who wants to touch them. Simply put, they have no "guts" when it comes to doing right.

Let's study some of the well-known ladies in the Bible to see what kind of faith and strength they had:

Rebekah

Rebekah possessed the faith to leave home, family, and everything she knew to marry and live with a perfect stranger because she recognized "God's will."

Noah's Wife

Noah's wife had the faith to leave behind family and friends, to get on the first ark ever made, to see it rain for the first time, and then to watch her loved ones drown because they would not listen.

Jochebed

Jochebed had the faith to place her baby boy in a basket made of bulrushes and leave him in the Nile River as the only hope of saving his life.

Sarah

Sarah had the faith to watch as her husband walked away with her only son to kill him as a sacrifice to God. (She did not know that God was going to spare his life!)

Esther

Queen Esther had the faith to put her life in danger and come before the king in order to save the lives of her people.

Ruth

Ruth had faith to leave behind the world she knew to live with her mother-in-law in a strange country.

Deborah

Deborah had the faith to go to battle with the soldiers and help defend her country against the enemies of God.

I don't believe these women (and these are just a FEW examples of women of faith in the Bible) were cowards when it came to standing for right! These women definitely had "guts" and a strong faith in the Lord Jesus Christ. And guess what?! Every time God came through for them and blessed them for their faith, He gave them much happier lives than they ever would have had if they had not put their trust in God, their strength. The Bible says in Psalm 18:32, *"It is God that girdeth me with strength...."*

There is a certain feminine strength that comes only from God. This fact does not make a woman hard and masculine but instead more beautiful and attractive. Guess what? Every guy who surrenders to serve God with his life needs a girl with strength and faith in a powerful, mighty God. It is true that "behind every great man stands a great woman." If you want a strong, Godly man, then you had better become a strong, Godly woman.

Each one of those young men who came forward on Friday night of Youth Conference, crying and surrendering to do God's will, will only do so if he has the right woman by his side. I challenge you today, dear reader, to be that woman—a woman of strength. Ask God to increase your faith, to draw you close to Him, and to cause you to never be afraid to stand for right.

> "Stand up, stand up for Jesus,
> Ye soldiers of the cross,
> Lift high His royal banner...."

Are you standing for Jesus? Are you standing for anything, or are you too weak to stand? Worse yet, are you bold in your stand against Christ?

Please trust me when I say that there will come a day when God will judge you, but you will have no strength to stand because He will force you to your knees. If you have been a coward or have been too afraid of what people may think of you if you take a stand for right, I beg you to start today. And guess where you learn how to stand? I think it is ironic that the best place to learn to stand up for Christ is down on your knees.

How to stand:

- ◆ Plug in to God!
- ◆ Plug in to Godly counselors!
- ◆ Pray for a Godly man!
- ◆ Practice doing right in the little things!

"EVERY ACTION OF OUR LIVES TOUCHES
ON SOME CHORD THAT WILL
VIBRATE IN ETERNITY."

–E. H. Chapin

"CULTIVATE ONLY THE HABITS
THAT YOU ARE WILLING
SHOULD MASTER YOU."

–E. Hubbard

CHAPTER SIX

Rahab or Rebekah

Two stories in the Bible show the vast difference between two girls who lived very different lifestyles, yet both were used by God to do something great. I'd like to share with you the stories of Rahab and Rebekah.

Rahab

Rahab was the town harlot who made her living by selling her body to men to do whatever they wanted. She would have been known today as a prostitute, a lifestyle that is still against the law in our country. So this woman was not exactly what we would call a virtuous woman or a woman of integrity. She was living a very wicked and ungodly life, yet God still used her to do an important job for Him.

54 | Real Love Can Wait

Joshua was preparing to conquer the city of Jericho and move in with his people, so he sent two spies to check out the land. The soldiers in Jericho soon learned of the presence of the spies and searched high and low for these men. The Israelite spies, desperate to save themselves, knocked at the door of Rahab and begged her to help them. She said she could and hid them under some straw on top of her roof! When the soldiers came knocking at her door a while later, they were not able to find the two spies. Rahab was responsible for saving the lives of those two men that day.

Before the spies left her house, Rahab begged them to ask Joshua to save her and her family. Since she had helped them, they promised to save her. She was to hang a red cord out of her window so the Israelite soldiers would know she was the one they were supposed to save. They had orders to leave her and her family unharmed. God protected her for the good deed she had done, and her life was spared, but He did record her in the Bible as Rahab, the harlot. God made sure that all of these hundreds of years later her lifestyle was written down for all to see and to know that God does not want us to be immoral in our living and that sin always comes with a high price.

Rebekah

Now let's turn to a girl named Rebekah, a very sweet, pure, innocent girl who grew up in a good family and who was taught the ways of God probably from a very young age. She was a hard worker and a servant who was preparing herself for the day when she would meet the one whom God had chosen for her.

One day she went, as she so often did, to draw some water from the nearby well. While there, she met one of God's messengers sent from Abraham to find a wife for his son Isaac. This servant of Abraham was waiting for a sign and had told God that the first girl to offer his camels a drink of water would be the one he would know was right for Isaac.

As Rebekah came to the well, she saw the messenger who asked her for a drink. She replied that she would not only give him a drink but would gladly give his camels a drink as well. He then told her who he was and explained his purpose in being at the well of water at that time. She invited him to meet her father and within a few days was on her way to meet a man she had never seen and with whom she would spend the rest of her life.

Talk about having faith! I'm not sure if I'd be that willing or brave, but God surely blessed her for her faith in Him. She became the grandmother to the 12 tribes of Israel and was in the lineage of Jesus Christ himself! God definitely used her to do some great and incredible things for Him. Now, I would imagine that at some point (probably after God spared her life!), Rahab turned to God and forsook her ungodly lifestyle, but her wicked living was definitely not what God had intended for her when He created her and gave her life. When she got right with God, she probably gave Him what she had left. God is so merciful that He always has another plan for our lives when we mess up the first one. Still, God does not want the leftovers of our lives; He wants, like Rebekah so beautifully illustrates, ALL of us.

Allow me to use a white sheet as an illustration of a person's life. God wants you to be completely pure, which is more than just not being physically immoral with a guy. He wants your heart pure, your mind pure, and your body, soul, and spirit pure. He wants everything you have, and when you refuse to give Him any part of you, you are defiling that part of your life and pretty much telling God that He is not allowed to have that part of you. When this happens, your life (the white sheet) begins to become dirty and marked by sin.

I have stayed in some pretty dumpy motel rooms at times, and there have been a few places where I have literally been afraid to sleep between the sheets for fear of what might be crawling under the covers! I remember being on a trip when we stopped in downtown St. Louis to see the arch where we stayed in a nasty hotel. We checked in and left promptly for a church service. When we returned, the police were there to investigate who had broken into the vending machines and stolen all of the items while we were gone!

We saw the pool and Jacuzzi covered in a layer of

grease, and the water was extremely dirty! Needless to say, we did not swim or sleep much that night, and we were more than ready to leave bright and early the next morning!

I would no sooner have taken those sheets off of those beds to use at my own house than I would go and find a mangy dog with fleas to sleep with me! That situation would not just be dirty; it would be disgusting! Yet, that is how our lives start to look when we slowly defile every part that God has given us with the filth and perversion of this world.

A girl may be a virgin physically, but perhaps her mouth is as filthy as those sheets were. Maybe she dresses right, but has no problem at all with watching immorality on television or video. Perhaps one teenager reads her Bible, but at the same time, she has hundreds of ungodly songs downloaded on her computer or I-pod that she justifies with the fact that she reads the Bible.

God sees everything, and He is the only One Who knows whether or not a person is truly pure in every area of life. Psalm 139:23 and 24 says, *"Search me, O God, and know my heart: try me, and know my thoughts: And see if there be any wicked way in me, and lead me in the way everlasting."* God wants you—all of you. Are you giving Him all of you today, or are you holding something back? God will use you when and only when you are willing to give Him everything you have and be completely pure and clean.

"YOU ARE TODAY WHERE YOUR THOUGHTS
HAVE BROUGHT YOU;
YOU WILL BE TOMORROW WHERE YOUR
THOUGHTS TAKE YOU."

–H. D. Thoreau

"THOUGHT IS ACTION
IN REHEARSAL."

–Anonymous

CHAPTER SEVEN

A Tender Heart

As a young girl, I used to love to listen to a certain Patch the Pirate song, and to this day, I love the song. The words go like this:

"Take me now, Lord Jesus; take me
    I would give my heart to Thee,
Thy devoted servant make me
    Only Thine to be.

Saviour, while my heart is tender,
    I would give Thee every part.
All my talents I surrender,
    I am Thine, Lord, here's my heart.

Use me now, Lord Jesus, use me
    As I tell of Calvary.

May Thy Spirit move within me,
  Leading souls to Thee."

My husband talked to the Hammond Baptist Junior High School students about a certain store where he does not like to shop because of the worldly influence it has on teenagers. He specifically told them he does not like the kind of clothing this store promotes and sells.

Well, we were on our way to an activity where we did some shopping, and some girls wanted to shop in this particular store. We shopped for a couple of hours, and after an hour, some girls came up to me and were worried about having gone into the store. They felt bad that they went in and did not want to get in trouble. After listening to them, I told them I was sure my husband would not be upset with them, and after they left, I thought about how sweet those girls are and what tender hearts they have. Even in the small decisions of their lives, they want to do right and please their authorities.

Not only is this kind of attitude what we look for when we choose someone to receive an award or an honor, but it is also an attitude that pleases God. So often teenagers develop an attitude of "I don't care what anyone says; I'll do what I want to." It is exciting to see teens with an open spirit and heart. The Bible says in Psalm 139:23, *"Search me, O God, and know my heart: try me, and know my thoughts."* God is looking for some teenagers to use who are open to Him.

Have you ever been somewhere where you felt totally out of place and you could not wait to get out of there? Todd and I started dating our freshman year of college. During the summer after our freshman year, his family decided to go to the Western Open. (For those of you who do not know, the Western Open is a golf tournament where professionals such as Tiger Woods play.) Well, Todd asked me to go with them, and of course, I was very excited. However, I had never met all of his family, so I was quite nervous too. Todd and his parents picked me up at my house, and then we all drove to the hotel where his family was staying. When we got there, we walked into one of the hotel rooms, and everyone was just sitting there staring at me. I said,

"Hi," and then my mind went blank. I could not think of anything else to say. All I kept thinking was, "How can I get out of here?"

The tournament was so fun, and I had a great time with everyone. (We even got close enough to Tiger Woods to reach out and touch him. I almost did, but I was too scared!) However, seeing Todd's family was awkward for me because I did not know them.

Can you remember how "out of place" you may have felt at the most awkward time in your life? Well, I believe that is how God feels when you are saved but never spend time with Him. It is as if He were living with a total stranger.

When I traveled on tour for Hyles-Anderson College, my tour group would often meet a designated family after the church service, ride home with them, and stay with them that night. They were always kind; but they did not know us, and we did not know them. We were polite to each other, but no one was willing to tell the other all of their heartaches and problems. They barely even knew our names—much less our life stories!

The more time you spend with God and the more you get to know Him, the more you see His heart and feel the love He has for you. The more you know Him, the more you will love Him, and the stronger your desire will be to please Him.

Sometime today or this week, write down the five people to whom you are closest. These are probably the five people you try to please more than anyone else. They are also the five people who have more influence in your life than anyone else. After you write down the names of these people, put "God" at the top. Then look at your list again and ask yourself, "If I try to please God, will I still be able to please these people?" If the answer is "yes," then you have the right influences in your life. If not, you need to make some new friends and get around some people who will help you to please God.

To have a tender heart for God means first of all, making sure you are a Christian, and secondly, it means spending time with Him. Thirdly, it means surrounding yourself with people who know Him and who also have a tender heart for Him.

Look at your list again and ask yourself, "Do I have a tender heart for God?" My mom has often said that she wants to live her life so that when she says, "I love You, God," He whispers back, "I know you do."

I know God loves me, and I hope He knows I love Him too.

CHAPTER EIGHT

How to Choose a Boyfriend

So in this chapter, let's talk about how to choose a boyfriend. Let me first tell you that it is always a good idea to ask for advice before you begin dating someone. I learned this lesson the hard way when I asked someone for permission to date a young man I had already begun dating. The person I talked to told me he strongly disapproved of my dating that particular guy. Oops! I would have saved myself a lot of hurt, misery, and tears if I had only gone for advice before I started dating this person.

There are, however, some guidelines that are given to us from, yes, the Bible, and even though the lifestyles of the people in those days were very different from ours in 2011, the truths have not changed and still apply to us today.

The Fool

The first example of who NOT to date in the Bible was the fool spoken of in Proverbs 7. He just wanted to please his woman, but he had no standards or convictions for himself. He was a simple man, meaning he just followed whichever way the wind blew and really was just not very smart. He probably would have been failing school if he went to one, and he also would probably not have cared if he was failing. He just had the total "I-don't-care" mentality—definitely not a good choice for a future mate!

Samson

Next there was Samson, a very strong, yet unsteady man. He would do right for a while; then a woman would come along whom he just could not resist, and he would backslide. Samson just could not stand up to the wiles of a woman! He was also a very selfish man. When he wanted something, he didn't care who he hurt or what he had to do to get it, but nothing was going to stand in his way. This type does not make for a very good husband (or boyfriend) since it takes a lot of giving in and unselfishness to make a relationship work.

Lot

And now we have Lot, a man who made foolish decisions. His failure to make wise decisions cost him his family. He was friends with the most vile members of society. He was a leader of a country that was destroyed for its immorality and perversion. Would you really want to fall in love and marry a guy whom your children would one day call a fool and would not even follow? I don't think so! Remember, love requires more than just a handsome face and a strong body.

Absalom

The rebel, Absalom, had a horrible relationship with his father, King David. Eventually he became so bitter, hateful, and vengeful that he tried to overthrow his father's kingdom by winning the hearts of the people and even tried to kill his own dad. Beware of guys who hate their fathers! Their lack of relationship with their fathers can cause many problems when they try to have a good relationship with their wives.

Hophni and Phinehas

The two sons of the priest (preachers' kids), Hophni and Phinehas, were so wicked in their heart that God killed them! Talk about giving preachers' kids a bad rap. These guys gave us preachers' kids no chance to redeem ourselves! They were extremely wicked in their minds, their hearts, and their actions. Obviously they were definitely not husband material.

Rehoboam

Rehoboam was a man who was too proud to get advice from his leaders. Do you know any guys like this? Avoid them at all cost!! Don't give them the time of day! How can someone lead you to a happy life if he won't follow the ones who are in charge of him? We are not born wise; we are supposed to get wisdom from those who have traveled further down the road of life than we have. Get advice and date someone who is willing to get advice too. You will be a whole lot happier if you do.

Judas

The last example is Judas Iscariot, the ultimate hypocrite. He looked the part, acted the part, and did the part until he just couldn't hide his sin anymore. He was supposed to be one of Jesus' closest friends until he stabbed him in the back and by turning Him in to the Roman guards. Talk about a horrible friend—he has to be one of the worst!

The "Judas" you know would be the one who everyone thought was a great teenager, but as soon as he graduated from high school, he immediately left church and all of the Christian friends he had made. He would become what he truly was all along, the partying, wild, drinking, immoral guy who loved the things of the world and was finally "free" from the "bondage" of standards, convictions, and Christianity. Just like Judas, who went out and killed himself after he realized what he had done to his friend, the guys who are now like him will one day realize that they really are not free at all but instead are captives in a prison of the miserable life they have chosen.

So now that you have an idea of the kind of guys to avoid, may I suggest some attributes that you should look for in a boyfriend and one day in a husband? If you will go through this "checklist" before you date a guy, I think you and he will be a lot happier, and you will be more likely not to choose a loser for a mate:

1	Do you admire him?
2	Does he encourage you to do right?
3	Is he respectful of authority?
4	Does he love God?
5	Does he try to protect your reputation?
6	Is he able to take a stand for right?
7	Would you want your daughter to date someone like him one day?
8	Is he good to his mother?
9	Does he have a good relationship with his father?
10	Does he treat you with respect?

These are just a few principles that I have learned along the way. These are questions my counselors would ask me when I was interested in dating someone or later when I was seriously thinking about marriage. I hope they will be a help to you because, apart from being saved, marrying the right man is the most important decision you will ever make.

"MATURITY IS LEARNING
HOW MUCH GOD LOVES YOU
AND LOVING OTHERS
IN THE SAME WAY."

–C. Schaap

CHAPTER NINE

If You Want to Be a Princess, You'd Better Marry a Prince!

At this writing, my husband Todd and I will celebrate our fifth wedding anniversary on June 1, and I can honestly say I am more in love with him today than I have ever been. I think he is even more handsome than when I met him (if that is possible), and the more I get to know him, the more I love and respect him.

I met Todd at a State Line Christian School soccer game during my senior year of high school. The first time I saw him, I immediately thought he was gorgeous, but we hardly talked. I think we said "Hello" and "Goodbye," and that was about it! The next time I saw him was at our basketball tournament in February of my senior year where we again said pretty much nothing to each other; yet, at that time, I became very interested in him. He was the MVP of our tournament and the star player of his team. I had a huge crush on him.

Well, I graduated and he graduated, and I had heard that he was writing to several girls from our school, so I did not think he was interested in me. I had some dates the summer after I graduated, but I could not get Todd Weber out of my mind. During that summer I decided to begin praying and fasting that God would show me whom to marry and that God would lead Todd Weber to Hyles-Anderson College if that was His will. At that time several colleges were recruiting Todd to play basketball. I had heard he was considering one in particular but was undecided as to what he would do. I saw him at Youth Conference, and we smiled at each other but did not talk.

During Youth Conference Todd decided that God wanted him to go to Bible college and serve Him. Todd followed his pastor's and parents' Godly counsel when he gave up his dream of becoming a basketball star.

He did come to Hyles-Anderson in the fall, and my brother Ken set us up on our first date. (The fact that Ken liked Todd was also a big plus!) Our first date was in September of 1999, but we did not begin to date on a regular basis until April of 2000 because Todd's youth pastor had advised him to wait. Todd, being the steady, strong type who always does the right thing, of course obeyed his youth pastor. I did not know his youth pastor had told him this though, so I thought he did not really like me. I dated around, but no one compared to Todd. I tried to get interested in someone but always found myself looking for Todd or comparing others to him, but no one ever measured up.

Finally in April we had a talk and soon began to date. We were engaged in October of 2001 and married on June 1, 2002. My parents' anniversary is also on June 1—though not the same year! We were married in the same auditorium in which my parents were married, and my dad performed the ceremony. It was a beautiful wedding and one of the happiest days of my life. I felt like a princess because I was marrying my handsome prince. Life was beautiful sunshine and roses, and we knew we would live happily ever after.

Five years later I am still living "happily ever after," yet all "happily ever afters" bring with them some struggles and sadness. In 2004 I found out that I was expecting our first child, only to find out a few months later I had miscarried. It was a very sad time in our lives, yet Todd was the perfect example of steadiness and strength, though I knew he was hurting too.

Todd has never been one to go on and on about things; he feels very deeply but keeps his thoughts and opinions to himself for the most part unless he is asked. During this time, his main concern was how I was doing and how he could best take care of me. He never even hinted that he was disappointed about losing our child.

However, several months later I was going through some papers in his office, and I found a note he had written me after the loss of our child. In the letter he said how much he loved me and hurt for me because I had to go through that pain. He said after I called him from the hospital, he got alone and cried for the child he would never see on this earth and prayed for me. When I read his letter, I wept and thanked God for giving me such a loving husband.

During our dating, I lost my grandfather who was also my pastor. It was a difficult time for my family as well as for our church; and while I was emotional, Todd was steady and strong, constantly telling me that everything would be okay.

We have had cloudy days and struggles, yet lots of sunny days and good times. Todd is my favorite person to be with, and he makes me laugh. He has a great sense of humor and is not so quiet once you know him. He is great with our junior highers, and he truly loves working with them. He wants each of them to succeed and is constantly thinking of ways to help them and love them. I admire my husband for many reasons, but the following are my top four:

- He is an outstanding father, and our children think he hung the moon.
- He is one of the hardest-working men I know, working long hours many times to get a job

done. (Thanks to his parents who taught him to work hard!)

- He is a deep thinker, a wise man, and one of the best Christians I know.
- He is, of course, a wonderful husband and my best friend.

At the time of this writing, Valentine's Day is coming soon, and I thought this holiday would be a good time to brag on my husband, but I also want to tell the teenage girls who are reading this chapter that your very own prince is out there somewhere. You may already be dating him, or you may not even know his name, but God will show you who he is in His time.

Don't get desperate and don't settle for less than God's best. I know there will be more hard times ahead and some more cloudy days, but knowing that I have someone to share with and help me make it through makes all the difference. I pray each of you will have your own "fairy-tale" wedding, marry your handsome prince, and live happily ever after with the man God chose for you.

CHAPTER TEN

Don't Marry a Fool!

(This Is Not a Personal Testimony!)

I only dated one person seriously before I met my husband, but like most of you who are teenagers, I was always interested in one or more guys! One of the reasons I did not date many guys for very long is I just grew tired of them. I remember one guy in particular whom I liked for a while, but he followed me around to make sure I did not talk to anyone else. His pursuit drove me crazy! I was insecure like most teenage girls, but because of a great home life as well as other reasons, I was not extremely insecure, nor was I looking for a person to fill a void in my life. As a result, I did not appreciate the over-protective type who was constantly "watching out" for me.

I liked many guys throughout my teenage years, and I had many guy friends, but when it came to looking for someone with whom to spend my life, the list became very small! I don't mean I had people standing in line to date me! I am sure I got on many people's nerves at times and probably drove some guys away with my "outgoing/annoying(?)" personality, yet there are some very specific characteristics I looked for as well as some characteristics I tried to avoid when I began to date seriously in college.

I recently read in Proverbs 7 about the married woman who talked a man into being immoral with her while her husband was out of town. Because that young man was simple, he did exactly what she asked him to do. Now, I would guess that this unfaithful wife and her husband did not have a great marriage, and I would have to blame her for the evil thing she did. (Evil is when you plan ahead to do something wrong. The Proverbs 7 woman was waiting for the young man to come by her house and planning to seduce him. Her intent was evil.) But the youth was definitely not innocent himself. I hope you realize that this man would not have been good husband material. If he was willing to take advantage of someone else's wife, he probably would not treat his own wife very well.

Let's talk about you and how in the world this story would possibly affect your life. I know it's an old Bible story and you are not yet married, but I think there are some important truths we can learn.

This Man Was Out Late Walking the Streets.

Most things that teenagers (or people in general, for that matter) do which they later regret happen late at night. I have found that the later it gets, the worse I get. If I stay up late talking to someone, the next day I am probably going to regret something I said.

When I lived at home, my parents always had a curfew for me. I had to be home by 10:30 or 11:00 p.m. at night. If you do not have a curfew, I would strongly suggest setting one—unless you are a better Christian than anyone I have ever met or talked to in my life!! People do not make big mistakes because they are "bad" people; most people make mistakes they will regret because they do not plan ahead.

He Went Into Her House Alone.

This is the reason why it is important to have chaperons. I am sure that the immorality level at our school and church would skyrocket if we did away with chaperons and let everyone single date. Most of the teenagers would be thrilled, I'm sure, as I would have been. However, ten years later, I think they would be shedding many unnecessary tears as they looked back at the mistakes they made and the people who were hurt.

My dad tells a story of a guy who came to college and began dating a girl. This guy did not see what was wrong with hugging and kissing before marriage. When he was getting ready to go home for the summer, my dad counseled with this young man and told him to be careful. He told my dad that he did not see how he could make it the whole summer without touching his girlfriend. My dad decided to help him, so he gave him a small two-sided picture frame to hang on his rearview mirror. One side of the frame had a picture of my dad; the other side had a picture of my grandpa, Dr. Jack Hyles, who was the pastor of our church at that time.

The young man went home for the summer. When he came back in the fall, my dad asked him how his summer went. He replied, "It was miserable! Every time I thought about touching my girlfriend, I would see that crazy picture frame spinning around and around. I didn't even come close to touching her all summer!" Well, he may have a had a miserable summer, but I am sure he is a happy man today!

He Did Not Have the Strength to Resist Her.

Everyone is tempted to do something he should not do at times because he is human. There is a strength however that helps you resist temptation which is found only through a close relationship with God. This guy did not have that strength because he made women more important than God.

"THE CHAINS OF HABIT ARE TOO WEAK
TO BE FELT UNTIL THEY ARE
TOO STRONG TO BE BROKEN."

–S. Johnson

"YOUR NAME IS WHAT YOU SAY YOU ARE.
YOUR REPUTATION IS WHAT FOLKS THINK YOU ARE.
YOUR CHARACTER IS WHAT GOD KNOWS YOU ARE."

–J. F. Hyles

CHAPTER ELEVEN

What Now?

So you have read this book and are thinking, "What now? I've already done the unthinkable and the unpardonable. I have already given away the most precious possession I have. There must be no hope for me."

Oh, but there is hope! There is always hope for you. As long as you are alive and breathing air, God has a plan for your life. Maybe it is not the original plan He had for you, but God is the God of second chances, and He always has a plan for your life.

One of the worst aspects of sin is the feeling of guilt and remorse that Satan immediately fills a person's soul with after the wrong is done. Satan is the master deceiver and the father of lies. He prides himself in convincing a person to commit a crime and then pouncing on that person like a cat and torturing her with feelings of regret and hopelessness. He wants nothing more than to destroy one's life. If the sin does not do that, he will try to make you tear apart your own life by making you feel like you are completely useless to God and that God cannot possibly use someone as wretched and vile as you…sound familiar? The worst thing you can possibly do is to give in to Satan's deceit and continue to make poor decisions because you feel you are not worthy of God's love and His grace.

I read a story about a girl who lost her purity as a teenager. She said that once she realized she had given herself away, she felt so filthy and dirty inside that she figured, "Why stop now?" She felt so hated by God and by her own self that she continued to consent to allowing guys to use her. Each time she drove herself further and further down into the pit of despair and hopelessness. It took her many years to realize that God loved her just as much as He loved the "pure" girls and that He still believed in her and wanted to use her to do something great for Him. The day she finally realized God's unconditional love for her was the day she quit giving herself away and turned to God for His true love and security.

I remember as a child getting punished for disobeying my parents. For a while they were upset with me and punished me, so the relationship we enjoyed was broken. Yet after the punishment was over and I had asked for forgiveness, we were closer than we had ever before been. I did not feel they hated me; I knew they loved me and still believed in me. It would have been crazy for them to disown me or to beat me or to tell me what a horrible daughter I was. That would not have fixed anything because disowning me, beating me, or berating me would have only made matters worse.

When we do something against what God says or when we commit a sin against Him, He does not disown us or try to hurt us. Yes, for a while there may be a punishment, and the relationship we had may become broken, but once the punishment is over, and we have asked Him for forgiveness, He forgives and forgets and loves us more than ever before. He is ever merciful. The Bible says in Lamentations 3:22, "...*his compassions fail not.*" He loves you—period. His unconditional love is not because of anything you have or have not done; He loves you because He chose to love you—because you are His.

I heard a girl who had grown up in a rough home with an unsaved family and who had been immoral with many guys talk about how she never realized that she was precious to God. She had no idea of the value He placed on her life; instead, she just thought she existed without anyone who really cared about her. She spoke about the first time she heard someone tell her that God loved her and that she was precious to Him. She said that realization changed her life and made her want to save herself for someone special who would love her like Christ loved her and who would value her life and her body as a precious gift from God. The moment she realized how important she was to God was the moment she stopped giving herself away and began the path to purity.

It is never too late to begin a life of purity. I love the statement, "Today is fresh with no mistakes in it." Once you have asked God to forgive you and have told Him how sorry you are, there should be no looking back. God is looking ahead at all of the wonderful possibilities in your future, and so should you. I would like to share some promises to claim from the Bible for those who are struggling with overcoming mistakes and moving ahead in life.

Psalm 37:26

"He is ever merciful, and lendeth; and his seed is blessed."

Psalm 116:1

"I love the LORD, because he hath heard my voice and my supplications."

Psalm 119:156

"Great are thy tender mercies, O LORD: quicken me according to thy judgments."

Proverbs 10:12

"Hatred stirreth up strifes: but love covereth all sins."

Lamentations 3:22, 23

"…because his compassions fail not. They are new every morning: great is thy faithfulness."

II Corinthians 12:9

"And he said unto me, My grace is sufficient for thee: for my strength is made perfect in weakness. Most gladly therefore will I rather glory in my infirmities, that the power of Christ may rest upon me."

Galatians 2:20

"I am crucified with Christ: nevertheless I live; yet not I, but Christ liveth in me: and the life which I now live in the flesh I live by the faith of the Son of God, who loved me, and gave himself for me."

Ephesians 1:7

"In whom we have redemption through his blood, the forgiveness of sins, according to the riches of his grace."

Hebrews 8:12

"For I will be merciful to their unrighteousness, and their sins and their iniquities will I remember no more."

Revelation 1:5

"And from Jesus Christ, who is the faithful wit-

ness, and the first begotten of the dead, and the prince of the kings of the earth. Unto him that loved us, and washed us from our sins in his own blood."

God loves us—unconditionally. I am so grateful for that because even the good things I do are in His sight as filthy and worthless as my sin. The only good about any of us is Jesus Christ. Please bask in His love, mercy, and grace today, and begin the journey to purity one step at a time. Yes, there will be struggles, and yes, times of pain and regret, but remember during the tough times that God is there holding you up, and *"underneath are the everlasting arms."* He loves you today, and He is crazy about you—never forget it!

Some Practical Steps to Beginning a Journey of Purity

1. Ask God to forgive you and make a commitment to purity. You may even want to go forward in your church and make your decision public.

2. Recruit help! Go to a Godly counselor or some counselors who can help you get on the right track and set up some safeguards to guide you along the way.

3. Get every guy you date approved by that counselor.

4. Do not go on unchaperoned dates. This will help you avoid temptations that you may face.

5. Do a Bible study on the words *mercy*, *grace*, and *love* which will help you realize your value to God.

6. Ask God every day to keep you pure and make sure you are spending daily time with Him.

7. Memorize verses about purity.

These are just a few ideas to help you stay on the right track. I wish you the very best, and I would love to help you in any way that I can! Please feel free to email me at tjweber02@att.net.

My Commitment to Purity

This commitment to purity form is your reminder about your decision to stay pure. You may want to copy it and give it to someone to whom you will be accountable. Ask the person to help you stay focused on your commitment. Allow that person to have veto power in your life. Trust that person to help you make the right decision on whom you will date.

I, _____, do make a holy vow to God to stay pure until my wedding day and to save myself for my husband.

Signed: _____

Date: _____

"If a man vow a vow unto the Lord, or swear an oath to bind his soul with a bond; he shall not break his word, he shall do according to all that proceedeth out of his mouth."

(Numbers 30:2)

The first step in making a commitment to purity is knowing for sure that you are on your way to Heaven. Being a child of God and having the help of the Holy Spirit to resist temptation and to set boundaries will help you keep your commitment. If you were to die today, are you 100 percent sure that you would spend eternity in Heaven? You need to realize the following:

- **Realize there is none good.** Romans 3:10 says, *"As it is written, There is none righteous, no, not one."*

- **See yourself as a sinner.** Romans 3:23 says, *"For all have sinned, and come short of the glory of God."*

- **Recognize where sin came from.** Romans 5:12 says, *"Wherefore, as by one man sin entered into the world, and death by sin; and so death passed upon all men, for that all have sinned."*

- **Notice God's price on sin.** Romans 6:23 says, *"For the wages of sin is death; but the gift of God is eternal life through Jesus Christ our Lord."*

- **Realize that Christ died for you.** Romans 5:8 says, *"But God commendeth his love toward us, in that, while we were yet sinners, Christ died for us."*

- **Take God at His Word.** Romans 10:13 says, *"For whosoever shall call upon the name of the Lord shall be saved."*

- **Claim God's promise for your salvation.** Romans 10:9-11 says, *"That if thou shalt confess with thy mouth the Lord Jesus, and shalt believe in thine heart that God hath raised him from the dead, thou shalt be saved. For with the heart man believeth unto righteousness; and with the mouth confession is made unto salvation. For the scripture saith, Whosoever believeth on him shall not be ashamed."*

Now pray. Confess that you are a sinner. Ask God to save you and receive Christ as your personal Saviour.